Cats

Cat Care
Kitten Care

How To Take Care Of And Train Your Cat Or Kitten

By Ace McCloud
Copyright © 2013

Disclaimer

The information provided in this book is designed to provide helpful information on the subjects discussed. This book is not meant to be used, nor should it be used, to diagnose or treat any medical condition. For diagnosis or treatment of any medical problem, consult your own physician or veterinarian. The publisher and author are not responsible for any specific health or allergy needs that may require medical supervision and are not liable for any damages or negative consequences from any treatment, action, application or preparation, to any person reading or following the information in this book. Any references included are provided for informational purposes only. Readers should be aware that any websites or links listed in this book may change.

Table of Contents

Introduction 6
Chapter 1 – Why A Cat Could Be The Purr-fect Pet For You 7
Chapter 2 – How to Choose a Cat 9
Chapter 3 – Kitten Care.. 12
Chapter 4 – Welcoming a Cat into Your Home................... 15
Chapter 5 – Cat Nutrition 18
Chapter 6 – Play Time for Cats 21
Chapter 7 – How to Train Your Cat and Understanding Cat Behavior 24
Chapter 8 – How to Keep Your Cat Healthy 27
Conclusion 29
My Other Books and Audio Books . Error! Bookmark not defined.

Be sure to check out my website for all my Books and Audio books.

www.AcesEbooks.com

Introduction

I want to thank you and congratulate you for buying the book, "Cat Care: Kitten Care- How To Take Care Of And Train Your Cat Or Kitten."

If you are a cat lover like me, then you know just how incredible cats can be as pets! This book contains proven steps and strategies on how to live in harmony with one of the greatest animals on the planet. In this book you will discover how to feed, play with, care for, and train your cats or kittens. The helpful tips and strategies discussed here will help ensure your cat's health, happiness and safety, so that you can enjoy the company of your furry friend for many years to come!

Chapter 1 – Why A Cat Could Be The Purr-fect Pet For You

Are you thinking of getting a pet? If you are like most people, you may be considering getting a dog, or perhaps goldfish or hamsters. But some people are just naturally drawn to cats. Cats as pets are extremely cuddly and cute when trained properly and they have an air of mystery and independence that many people find irresistible. Let's look closely at the reasons why a cat might be the ideal pet for you.

Cats are very charming creatures. If you have looked deeply into their enigmatic eyes, stroked their soft fur, and heard their adorable purring, you will understand why they are such endearing little things.

Cats are ideal for people who are looking for quiet companionship. They are not as noisy and demanding as dogs. They don't run around much, making a mess or demanding your attention. If quiet relaxation is what you crave, you can count on getting just this with a pet cat, more so in their later years than when they are young. Most cats will quietly just sit around as you read, cook, do needlework or type on the keyboard. As such, cats tend to be preferred by people who are into crafts, cooking, gardening and other quiet, home-based activities. Dogs, meanwhile, are better suited for people who are into fishing, hunting, camping, running and other active hobbies.

Cats are also very loyal. Despite what you may have heard, dogs are not the only pets who are devoted to their owner. There is, however, some truth to the opinion that with cats, you have to first "earn" their loyalty, in a matter of speaking. Cats may not immediately show their affection or devotion, but once they know who feeds them and takes care of them, they give this person their complete loyalty. When this happens, they can be very affectionate pets. A sign of this affection is when a cat snuggles and rubs against your legs and feet, just when you least expect it. Another sign is when they just lie quietly in your lap, purring softly, as if to say, "You're not alone, I'm here no matter what." These are some of the joys of being a cat owner.

Cats, like some dogs, are fluffy and warm. If you want a pet that you can stroke, cuddle and bond with, go for a cat. You can't do this as much (or at all) with fish and birds.

Cats can live a long time. They can be your companion for as long as twenty years, maybe even more, especially if they are kept indoors. Hamsters, guinea pigs, rabbits and other small animals have a much shorter lifespan. If longevity is a concern, a cat would be the better option. Parents who are thinking of getting a pet for their children should give this some thought. It can be very devastating to have a pet die on you, and nobody wants their child to go through this experience.

Cats can also coexist peacefully with other pets in the household, provided you make the effort to properly train all your pets to live together. Despite the stereotype, cats and dogs can be quite good friends. Even cats and fish can live together, as long as the fish are safely kept in an aquarium that the cat can't reach. Some animal experts, however, caution against getting a cat when you already have a bird. The cat could end up hurting the bird. But of course, there are ways to work around even the most challenging situations if you are motivated enough. Many pet owners manage to keep both cats and birds with few problems.

Finally, cats are interesting companions. They act like "normal" pets most of the time, but at other times, they act as if nobody owns them. They can be their own boss, strutting around the house as if they own the place and entirely ignoring their owner (and all humans for that matter). For some people, this can be irritating, but for most cat lovers, it is an endearing trait. It's just how cats are: warm and affectionate most of the time, yet also proud, independent and infinitely more fascinating than dogs will ever be.

Chapter 2 – How to Choose a Cat

Deciding to have a pet cat is just half of the story. The other half is choosing the type of cat that's just right for you. There are a lot of questions to answer, such as should you get a kitten or a grown cat? Should you choose a cat with short hair or a cat with long hair? Which breed or species? Male or female? What color? How many cats should you choose?

The answers are purely subjective, of course, conforming to your personal tastes. If you are undecided, you can look at some cat pictures online and see what takes your fancy, or you can visit a pet shop or animal shelter.

Another thing to consider in choosing a cat is your own lifestyle. Do you have enough time to care for a young kitten? Would you enjoy playing with it and devoting time to training it? Do you simply want to have a cat around as a companion? These kinds of questions will help you decide if you want a cat that's docile or active, purebred or mixed-bred, furry or short haired (long-haired cats will require a lot of grooming), and so on.

Here are some considerations to think about:

- Kittens require more care and attention than adult cats. Kittens are also more playful and energetic. You will need to take the time in their early years to play with them and train them so that in a few years they are the perfect companion. They are also likely to change in both appearance and personality as they grow older, so what you see now may not be what you will get after a few years. If a cat's looks are important to you, consider getting an adult cat or at least a cat eight months or older.

- If you want a cat that's quiet and calm, get an adult cat instead of a young one.

- If there are little children at home, be sure to teach them the proper ways to hold and pet a cat. Young children, even with the best intentions, tend to be rough on pets, although cats are very tough, and nothing can bring as much joy as cute little kittens to children. Also, keep in mind, that no matter what pet you get, children should be supervised around pets until they know how to properly treat them.

- Keep in mind that the whole family will be involved when you get a pet cat. If anyone has allergies to cats, you may need to rethink your plan of getting a cat, or you can get a cat that has been genetically modified to take away the allergen that makes many people allergic. These cats are rare and very expensive though.

- Cats are like people with their own personalities. Even sibling cats are different from one another. If possible, choose a cat with a personality that will fit into your household. Ask its previous owner, or the pet shop owner, or the worker at the animal shelter if the cat you wish to get is calm and easy-going, or if it pretty much prefers to be left alone. Friendly cats will tolerate being handled, while others don't like to be handled as much. If you train a cat while it's young to be picked up a lot, it will definitely make a big difference when the cat is grown. Active cats like to explore around (hence they need more living space), while lazy, Garfield types will prefer to eat and nap all day.

- Cat personality is partially influenced by breed. Exotic breeds like Bengal cats are very active, Persian cats are usually calm and quiet, and Siamese cats tend to make a lot of meowing noises. If you want a purebred cat, read up on this topic. Also be prepared to spend more money for its purchase and be aware that purebreds generally don't live as long as other cats. Also be aware that some cat breeds are predisposed to certain medical conditions as well. If you are not picky about breed, go for mixed-breed cats. They tend to be healthier than purebreds.

- Special-needs cats require more attention, but taking care of them can be a very rewarding experience. A cat that is deaf or blind is able to give as much affection and companionship as any other cat. Similarly, cats that are older or that are suffering from some life-long illness may just be what brings more love and tenderness into your home. If you decide to get a special-needs cat, be sure you can provide the extra attention and medical care they need.

- I recently got three cute kittens a little over a year ago. I went to the local animal shelter and was shocked at how many cute little kittens they had. There were many more kittens at the animal shelter than at the local pet store and they were about 75% cheaper as well. Going to a local animal shelter not only can save you a lot of money, but many times you can have an incredible selection as well. Also, you get that warm fuzzy feeling of saving an animal that may have been put to death otherwise. If cats are not spayed and neutered, they can breed quite rapidly. I chose three cute kittens from the same litter, the two males were orange and white and black and white, and the female was a calico. If possible, choosing kittens from the same litter will ensure them a much higher chance of getting along with each other throughout their lives. Getting these kittens all together from the same litter was one of the best choices I ever made. They are super cute, get along well with each other and since I had plenty of time to train them, they are very well behaved and love to be around people. They also love to play with each other, so I don't have to play with them as much if I don't feel like it. Another thing to keep in mind is that two female cats not from the same litter will have a much higher chance of not getting along with each other.

Chapter 3 – Kitten Care

Kittens are such cute, furry little mini-me's of cats. They are so tiny, little, and full of life. Many people instantly fall in love with their new kitten. However, raising a kitten is a little different from raising an adult cat. Since kittens are not fully developed, they often require some special attention and different needs. Kittens are more prone to developing skin problems or other diseases as well as fleas. They are also more likely to get into trouble, so it is crucial to know how to care best for it. This information is especially important to know if you've found wild kittens and you want to rescue them, although you can apply it to just about any kitten.

Newborn Kittens. Newborn kittens should stay with their mother until they are at least 6 weeks old. The milk from their mother provides them with important antibodies and nutrients for healthy growth. Also, kittens this young cannot keep themselves warm, so they must rely on the body heat of their mother and siblings to stay warm. If you have found abandoned kittens at this age, there are some special steps that you must take to ensure that they stay healthy. If a kitten is under 4 weeks old, it is crucial to bottle-feed it once every two hours. You should also pay attention to its urinary patterns. Kittens this young should be kept in a box or crate with plenty of blankets or warm bedding. A good idea is to consult with a vet when you are dealing with kittens this young. Many kittens that are found in the wild are more prone to developing eye infections and other diseases.

At about a week to 10 days old, kittens should be able to open their eyes. Most kittens' eyes are blue at birth but will change after 3 months. Once they are 3 weeks old they will start to stand and crawl around. After those milestones, their development will begin to accelerate and they will start growing into their motor skills, hunting skills, and other adult features.

Weaning Your Kitten. Many kittens are ready to start eating formula and kitten food after about 5 weeks. If you're bottle-feeding, you can tell when a kitten is ready if it starts to forcefully bite the nipple of the bottle and/or when it is able to lick from your fingers. When this occurs, you can start the transition by allowing the kitten to lap formula from a spoon. When the kitten has proven to be able to do this, you can start to put its food in a dish. Don't be afraid to continue bottle-feeding during the weaning process if your kitten is not eating enough on its own. You don't want to starve it. Gradually work with your kitten until it is able to eat without the bottle. Start with moist food, as many kittens cannot chew hard food until they are at least 8 weeks.

Kittens Between 8 and 11 Weeks. Kittens between 8 and 11 weeks old begin to develop their motor skills, meaning they will start to run around and play more. Since your kitten will be more likely to want to explore, it is important to keep a good eye on it. Don't allow your kitten of this age to wander around your house yet, especially if you live in a big home. A good idea is to confine it to a smaller room (maybe a guest bedroom or spare bathroom) and let it explore there until it gets a little bigger and used to its environment. Also, kittens of this age can begin to eat kitten food as they will not need their mother's milk anymore.

Kittens Between 2 and 4 Months. During this age range, your kitten will be very energetic. You should feed your kitten at least 3 times a day, ensuring that each serving contains at least 30% protein as recommended by the ASPCA. Since your kitten will start to really grow during this stage, you can begin to allow it to explore the rest of your house. I have had cats throughout my whole life and have found it much easier to just put down a bowl of dry food and a water bowl and keep them filled all the time. Cats are very smart and will stop eating when full, unlike some dogs. I will also feed my cats one serving of wet cat food per day. I used to have a cat that insisted on only eating wet cat food, and later in her life she had terrible tooth decay problems, so it is generally best to have the majority of the food dry cat food.

Kittens Between 4 and 6 Months. Since your kitten is close to becoming an adult cat at this point, it is a good idea to consider getting them spayed or neutered. This is because he or she will begin to develop the stages of sexual maturity. Getting this done can help you avoid spraying issues or ending up with more kittens than you've bargained for. If you are looking for a quiet cat, then be sure to get this done! Cats that have not been spayed or neutered can be quite a handful!

Litter Box Training. It is important to begin training your cat to use a litter box as early as possible to avoid accidents around the house. Kittens learn how to use the bathroom when their mother licks their rear end, which stimulates their bladder and rectal functions. If you've rescued kittens, you can do this yourself by gently rubbing those areas and its lower stomach with a moist towel or cotton tissue. If done right, it should make your kitten want to urinate. It should also relieve its bowels once a day. A good age to begin training your kitten to use a litter box is 4 weeks, as it will be old enough to learn. The trick is to put your cat in its litter box after every time it eats. Usually they will catch on themselves and you don't have to do much. If your kitten doesn't respond to the litter box, you can gently take its paw and stimulate a scratching in the litter. When I have new kittens, the first thing I do is put them in the litter box like five times in a row and then a bunch of times after that. They usually catch on pretty quick.

Keeping Your Kitten Clean and Healthy

Preventative care is very important when you have a kitten. This includes bringing it to the vet, keeping it clean and flea-free, and getting it vaccinated. It is important to make an appointment with your vet as soon as possible so that he or she can check the kitten to make sure it doesn't have any skin irritations or other problems, like ear mites. Your vet can also administer important vaccinations to prevent rabies, distemper, and leukemia. Taking your kitten to the vet is also a great way to let it learn how to socialize.

In terms of cleaning, mother cats often teach their babies how to groom themselves by licking their fur. If you've rescued kittens, you can stimulate this by using a damp towel to wash them, using short strokes as if it were their mother's tongue. If you've rescued a kitten, it is important to check their ears for dirt and other infections, such as mites. You can do this by simply using a cotton swab. One major sign of ear mites is dirt that looks like coffee grounds.

How To Eliminate Fleas From Kittens

It is important to monitor your kitten for fleas, otherwise they may develop anemia, which can be life-threatening. If your kitten has fleas, the first thing you can do is brush its fur using a special flea comb. You should also spray it with a kitten-safe flea spray. Once you've sprayed it, let it sit on an old towel in the bathtub for about 15 minutes or so to catch any dead fleas. Throw the towel away afterward. Once the dead fleas are off the kitten, you should give it a bath using special soap, something gentle. Dish soap that is not antibacterial often works well. Be sure to use warm, room-temperature water. Comb out its fur again and then gently dry it.

Bonding With Your Kitten

Once you have taken care of the important health logistics for your kitten, next comes the fun part: giving it as much love and attention as you can. Be sure to pet your kitten often and allow it to snuggle with you, something that your kitten will carry over into adulthood. Groom it regularly to prevent any hair or skin problems. It will also feel great to your kitten. Buy some kitten-safe toys and set up a playtime to help your kitten bond with you and hone its natural hunting instincts. Playtime is also important to strengthening your cat's motor skills, as you will learn in a couple of chapters. Once your kitten has hit 6 weeks and has received the proper vaccinations, you can allow it to interact with other cats and even dogs if they're cat-friendly. Reward your kitten with kitten treats to reinforce good behavior and help build confidence. Finally and most importantly, always be patient with your kitten and encourage good behavior (for example, no biting or scratching). A water bottle is the ideal deterrent for unwanted behavior. If you follow these steps, you are likely to create an unbreakable friendship for the rest of your cat's life.

Chapter 4 – Welcoming a Cat into Your Home

When you first bring a cat home, have these essentials ready: cat food, water, litter box, cat scratching post (the ones made of cardboard work really good), a few toys and a cat brush. For an extra treat, take some catnip and sprinkle it on the scratching post or cardboard.

It's also recommended that you prepare a so-called "isolation room" for your new pet. It can just be a corner in a room if you don't have much free space. This isolation room is where your cat will spend its first few days in its new home. It's important that this room be kept quiet—or at least as quiet as the circumstances will allow. Of course, you will all be excited about the new pet; if there are children in the household, they will fuss over it. Allow everyone to get to know the new cat(s), but give it space too. A kitten can be timid and easily frightened, as are some adult cats too. Watch over your new cat(s), but allow it some breathing space as well.

In the isolation room, provide a bed, food and water bowls, litter box and perhaps a few toys and a scratching post. Make sure to keep the litter box some distance away from the bed and food. You wouldn't want to eat right next to where you defecate, and your cat surely feels the same. But don't situate the litter box too far away that your cat can't find it. A distance of about six feet between the food bowl and the litter box should be sufficient. You can even shorten this distance if your pet is just a small kitten. Finally, make sure that the litter box is placed in a quiet and not-too-exposed spot. Your cat values its privacy, just like you do.

After about two weeks, when your cat appears to have settled in, allow it to go outside the isolation room and explore the rest of the house, a bit at a time. A good indication that it has settled in is when it is eating well and using the litter box, and when it doesn't hide from people. When the cat explores outside the isolation room, keep the rest of the house as quiet as possible so as not to alarm it. If it hears loud noises or sees a lot of movement (for example, from children running around), it may feel frightened and retreat to its room. Explain to children in the house that they need to tone things down to avoid scaring the new addition to your family.

Now, you may be curious as to what to feed your new cat, and how to do it. We shall devote a whole chapter to this important topic. Before we go into that, here are some more things you can do to ensure the safety of your cat when it first moves in:

- Ensure that your cat stays indoors unless you want to have an indoor/outdoor cat. It is possible to train a cat to walk with a harness type leash, but this is usually not recommended. It is wise to carry your cat around the outside of your house in your arms so that they know their surroundings. Be sure to hold your cat in an upright position when doing this, as this will make them feel more confident. You want to walk around your property several times per day for at least a week. Once a cat knows where they live, they are generally smart enough to return home over and over again, and it greatly reduces the chances of them getting lost if they do get out of the house. I had a friend who never let her cat out, and one day the cat broke out through an improperly fastened screen window and immediately got lost and she never saw him again. When letting your cat outside on its own the first few times, it's a good idea to go out with them. With my three new kittens I went out with them each time the first few weeks, letting them know the house boundaries, keeping them from climbing trees and then bringing them back inside (often times they want to stay outside and play.) It can be very stressful letting your cats outdoors, but nothing in the world will give them more joy. You can also install a cat door, which will allow your cats to go inside and outside whenever they want. My cats now go outside every day and they love playing in the forest. When you need to travel or go to the vet, be sure to use a cat carrier.

- Keep your house cat-safe. Ensure that windows are screened and doors are kept closed so that your cat cannot get out accidently. Also, make sure that spaces in the house that they might inadvertently crawl into are closed or sealed. In particular, keep drawers, closets, washers, dryers, ovens and other appliances closed to prevent your cat from climbing inside and becoming trapped there. Before closing a cabinet or drawer, look inside first to check if a kitty is hiding there. I had a cat once that climbed into an open air vent, and it was quite the ordeal to get her out!

- Provide a collar with an ID for your cat. The ID should have your name, address and contact numbers, plus your cat's name. Should your pet manage to go outside without your knowledge, or should it become lost, the finder will know how to return it through the information in the ID. You can also have the vet install a microchip in your cat, which has all of the important details available for scanning if your cat is found and brought to a shelter.

- Groom your cat by brushing their fur regularly. Apart from making your cat look its best, this will help make its skin and fur healthy. I recommend the shed ender brush. It only costs like six bucks and is by far the best cat brush I have ever seen. Bring your cat to a grooming clinic if you need to, if only to see how the process is properly done so that you can do it at home the next time. Grooming your cat yourself is a good way to bond with your pet. Sometimes, however, you need to have a professional do it, especially when the cat's fur is all matted up and may need to be shaved off or when it has skin breaks or lumps that also need to be treated.

- Regularly clean the cat's litter box. At least once every day, scoop the box. Also, wash it regularly before putting in fresh cat litter, using dishwashing liquid and warm water.

- Bring your cat to the vet for regular check-ups and inoculations. This is also a good time to ask the vet about any health concern you may have concerning your pet. Also talk to the vet about possibly spaying or neutering your cat. This is good for its health and it will also help prevent cat overpopulation. A cat that is not spayed or neutered can be twice as hard to handle as one that is.

- De-clawing your cat is an option for indoor cats, but it is something I would never personally do. If you let your cat outdoors, your cat should not be de-clawed. While a cat may do some damage to a few pieces of furniture in the beginning, you should be able to train them quite easily not to scratch the furniture, especially if you have a nice scratching post with catnip on it. A cat's claws are its main defense and I always find it a bit sad when a cat has been declawed.

Chapter 5 – Cat Nutrition

Now comes the all-important question of what to feed your cat. Basically, cats need fresh water and a nutritious, balanced diet. However, there is much more to this process beyond the realms of dry or canned cat food.

How you feed your cat ultimately determines its life expectancy. Similarly, how you feed yourself reflects your own life expectancy. There are many negative things that can happen if your cat's diet is poor. This is often reflected by a dry, thin coat of fur. Moreover, a poor diet can lead to obesity, which often leads to diseases such as arthritis, heart disease, liver disease, and kidney disease. It can also lead to dental issues, poor nail growth, stomach problems, respiratory or bladder problems, and an overall poor immune system.

It may seem like the cat food you use has your cat's diet covered, but the truth is that sometimes the marketing used on the package can be deceitful. Cat food packaging often claims that "cats love the taste" or that it is packed with nutrition but it is important to know the components of a healthy cat diet so you can make wise decisions for your furry friend.

Your cat's diet should consist of 6 key ingredients: protein, carbohydrates, fats, vitamins, minerals and water. Cats need a high-protein diet and the best source is food that is made from muscle meat. Many commercial, big brand cat foods use plant-based proteins, which are not as healthy. Your cat also needs carbohydrates, which you can find in fruit and vegetable sources. Avoid any kind of food that uses grains. Fats are important because they act as your cat's main source of energy. They are important for skin health and they help your cat's body absorb vitamins, which help process food. Many commercial cat foods use synthetic vitamins, which are not as healthy as natural vitamins. Minerals are also important for your cat's functioning, although the needs of minerals will differ from cat to cat. Finally, as you know, your cat needs water to stay hydrated. Interestingly, cats prefer to drink from a running water source, so if possible you should let them drink from a faucet or a small fountain.

When it comes to purchasing cat food and picking a diet for your cat, there are some important things that you should take into consideration. The worst types of cat food are the semi-moist kind (they often can be bought in pouches.) Semi-moist food is like junk food for cats and is not recommended by health experts.

Canned cat food is a better option because it contains a decent ratio of protein to carbohydrates. Just remember that too much canned food can lead to dental problems later on. When it comes to canned food, it is best to avoid commercial, big brand names and opt to go for ones that are manufactured by small, private companies, as they tend to use more natural ingredients. Another option is to put your cat on a home-based diet, meaning that you prepare its meals using fresh meats such as chicken or turkey. There is also the raw food diet, which utilizes raw ingredients. You can purchase raw foods for cats at high-end pet stores or you could allow your cat to find its food on its own (such as by catching mice).

If you opt to feed your cat using ready-made pet food, it is important to know how to read the label. If you see any of the following words in the ingredients section on cat food, avoid buying it at all costs:

- Corn syrup, salt, propylene, glycol, potassium sorbate, BHT, BHA, propyl gallate, ethoxquin, sodium nitrate, red/blue/yellow dyes, poultry by-products, meat by-products, artificial flavoring, oats, bran, rice, germ, soybean, sugar, or sorbitol

Also, it is important to be aware of price. When it comes to cat food, you get what you pay for. If you're paying $5 for cat food, odds are the ingredients will not be very healthy. Your cat is probably very important to you so don't be afraid to spend a little more money on its diet.

Depending on what diet you choose for your cat, you may consider using dietary supplements. It's not a bad idea but you should certainly consult with your vet to make sure that it is the right thing for your cat. Holistic vets are often very knowledgeable when it comes to cat supplements. A good idea is to start by researching the company who manufactures your cat's favorite food to see if they are missing any key ingredients.

Finally, you may end up switching your cat's diet. When doing this, the most important thing is to be patient. When your cat starts eating new food, it will cause its body to detox. The slower your cat's body detoxes, the better. If it detoxes too fast, your cat may get sick. A good way to transition your cat from old food to new is to start by mixing both together. Once a week, gradually add more and more new food and less of the old food. This can be a very long process, depending on which diets you're switching too (for example, a cat going from dry food to canned won't need as long as a cat going from canned to a home-based diet). Depending on the diet, give your cat at least 2 to 6 months to get used to the new food.

As always, consult with your vet on what you should do in terms of your cat's diet. Your cat may have special needs depending on its current health. Here are some other basics of cat nutrition that you should know when it comes to feeding your pet:

- By nature, cats are strict carnivores. For optimum health, they need meat and animal-based proteins. A lot of commercial cat foods contain plant-based protein (coming from grains and vegetables), which is cheaper but not ideal for cats.

- Canned food is better for your cat than dry kibble. Dry food is inferior because it tends to have very low water content, very high carbohydrate content, and plant-based rather than animal-based protein. Even though your cat may appear healthy enough eating only dry food, it is very likely it's not getting enough nutrition. There is a chance that problems may arise later on, as certain cat diseases are associated with an exclusively dry food diet. These potential problems include diabetes, kidney disease, obesity, and dental issues. I give my three cats one can of wet cat food split between them in the morning, and then they will eat dry cat food the rest of the day.

- Always provide fresh water together with the cat food, in a separate bowl. Always see to it that your cat gets enough water, especially on dry days. Replenish its water bowl as needed. It is a good idea to *always* keep the water bowl filled, so that your cat can drink whenever it feels thirsty.

- Do not give bones to your cat. These will likely splinter into small, sharp pieces that can get caught in your poor cat's throat.

- Do not feed your cat with dog food! Strangely enough, some pet owners do this. What's good for one species of pets is not good for another species.

- If your cat does not finish its meal of moist food within two hours, refrigerate it. Or just throw it away. Moist food gets spoiled much faster than dry food.

- When testing new cat food, buy small amounts at first to discover what your cat prefers. Cats can be very picky, so buying six different cans of cat food to find out which ones they like will save you a lot of hassle in the future.

- Food and water bowls made of metal, ceramic and glass are preferable to plastic. Plastic material can be scratched, and this creates a breeding space for harmful bacteria.

- Cat treats are a big favorite by nearly all cats. They can be used to train your cat in a variety of things. They are also great for getting a cat to come to you at important times. Just shake the treat bag and they will usually come running. However, it is important to note that cat treats should not make up more than 10% of your cat's diet. Temptations cat treats is a huge favorite for my cats.

Chapter 6 – Play Time for Cats

Play is an essential part of a cat's routine. It is a valuable source of exercise and great for when you want to bond with your cat. Most importantly, playtime allows your cat to practice its natural hunting skills. Further, it can help your cat release aggression and stress, boost its confidence and it is good for when a cat is transitioning into a new home. If you find that your cat is acting up or behaving badly, it usually means that you are not giving it enough play time.

When it comes to cat playtime, there are two different types of play that your cat can engage in—interactive and solo. Interactive play occurs when both you and your cat play together. For example, if you had a wand toy with a string and attached target and you used it to play with the cat, this would be interactive play. Solo play is when your cat plays with its toys by itself. Good ways to promote solo play are to place toys around the house where your cat might find them in its curiosity. Other cats are also great, as they can find great entertainment in playing with each other if they are around the same age.

Make sure that you provide your cat some toys and a scratching post. Cat toys need not be expensive. In fact, you can find stuff around the house that your cat will enjoy playing with for hours on end. For example, you can just crumple some paper into a ball and give it to your cat, and he will find it endlessly fascinating. Other suggestions are using ping-pong balls (make sure they are not broken), open paper bags (without the handle), and balls of yarn. My cat's favorite toy is a piece of rope that I flick in and out of their reach, or make them jump high in the air to reach. I used to use string, but one of my cats got in the bad habit of eating the string, so I found a slightly thicker piece of rope works much better. Also, feathers at the end of a long plastic handle are a favorite as well. Rotate the toys so that your cat will not be bored. You can also visit a pet shop and inquire about available toys for cats.

A nice place for your cat to hang out and be entertained on his own is by a window overlooking the street or garden. Make this window perch accessible and your pet will appreciate it. I keep my windows open all the time, with the screen down of course, and my cats just love to sit there and see what is going on outside. I also will take a handful of birdseed and sunflower seeds and throw it outside the screen door, and my cats especially love watching all the birds and squirrels that come to eat it.

You can also buy a cat tree or kitty condo. This is a structure that your cat can climb and perch on. The trunk and branches of the cat tree are usually covered in carpet or a rough material called sisal that cats enjoy scratching.

One really fun game that you can play with your cat is to use a wand toy and let the cat go "hunting." Get the cat's attention by putting the end of the toy on the floor and stringing it along, varying your speed. When you see your cat crouch down and ready to pounce, that is a sign that he or she is exercising its hunting skills. You can pull the toy away from the cat's reach a few times but always make sure that you let it win eventualluy. This helps build confidence.

Sometimes a cat doesn't usually need much to be entertained. It also likes spending many hours alone doing nothing. But remember that you need to play with it too. It will appreciate your presence more than any toy you can provide. Playtime is the perfect time to bond with your pet and get to know one another. If you notice your cat is being especially bad, it is usually because you are not playing with it enough and tiring it out. Playtime is especially important if your cat doesn't have any other cats around the same age to play with.

More Tips on Play Time With Your Cat

- Put the toys away after playing, otherwise your cat may lose interest in them
- Let your cat set the pace of playtime
- Don't make the games too easy but always let the cat win
- Allow cats to play together if you have several of them
- Give out treats after a good, hard play session
- Stop playing for 10 to 15 minutes after your cat has won
- Stop playing if your cat is not into it after a few minutes
- Don't use your hands as toys—that can encourage biting or scratching
- Don't pin or wrestle your cat
- Don't put toys in your cat's face—let it hunt
- Don't end playtime suddenly—have a cool down session

Fun Toys For Playing With Your Cat

Cat Dancer 301 – This is a fun toy for encouraging your cat to get some exercise by jumping around and chasing after the string on this toy. It is great for interactive play.

Smart Cat 3833 Peek-A-Prize Pet Toy Box – This really cool puzzle game is great for encouraging cats to play on their own. You can hide your cat's favorite toys in this box and then let them try to get them out themselves. It's really handy for keeping cats busy, especially when they're the kind that likes to get into everything.

Play-N-Squeak MouseHunter – This is another great toy that can be used for solo play and it looks just like a real mouse so it is bound to keep your cat busy for a while. This toy can be useful for encouraging your cat to bring out its natural hunting instincts and it comes with catnip to keep him or her really entertained.

SmartyKat CrackleChute Collapsible Tunnel - This small tunnel makes a crackling sound with every step of your cat's paw, which most cats really love. It's a really good toy for when you have several cats, as they like to chase each other through it. Kittens also really seem to enjoy this toy.

Go Cat Catcher Teaser Wand With Mouse – This is another great interactive toy that cats love. You and your cat can have hours of fun with this toy as you drag the mouse along and watch your cat try to catch it.

Also be sure to check out the cat toys at your local pet store, as they may have a more unique selection.

Chapter 7 – How to Train Your Cat and Understanding Cat Behavior

You must train your cat to first of all, do essential things like using the litter box and not scratching up the furniture. Afterwards, you can train it to do other nice-but-not-that-essential things like coming when its name is called and not jumping up on the kitchen counter. I have trained my cats to jump in the air and gently bat my hand with their paw to let all the treats fall out.

The secret to essential cat training is establishing a routine and placing things properly. As mentioned earlier, you should not place the litter box right next to the food bowl. Provide some distance between the two or the cat will not be very eager to use either one of them. Also, make sure that there's always a water bowl next to the food bowl. And do not move things around once your cat has become accustomed to the layout.

For the litter box, you can buy one from a pet shop, or simply use a standard open pan. You can use a covered box if you are concerned with odor. You can also put a mat under the box to minimize litter being scattered on the floor and around the room. Keep the box clean, scoop cat feces out at least once daily, and sweep any scattered dirt in the room. As much as possible, the litter box should be in a quiet, private place just for your cat, away from children and other pets. If you have more than one cat, it is recommended to have at least one extra litter pan.

You may need to experiment with various kinds or brands of litter to find which one your cat prefers. When you have discovered his favorite, stick to it. Stock up on this type of litter so you won't run out.

Understanding a cat's natural behavior also helps in training. By nature, cats are creatures of habit and they don't like change. Cats are also fastidious animals, so remember to always clean the litter box. If it's not clean, your cat may not use it all.

Training your cat to eat on time is not as complicated. Just place food in their bowl during meal times: three times a day at breakfast, lunch and dinner. Remember to fill his water bowl too. Observe regular meal times to establish the daily routine. Unlike dogs, which will overeat if given the opportunity, cats are smart enough to stop eating when full. It is not necessary to have feeding times. You can simply just keep their dry cat food bowl full, and they will eat at their own leisure. This is especially nice if you have to leave them alone for a day or two. Simply make sure you have lots of food and water down, and they will be fine.

Train your cat to stop doing unwanted things like scratching the furniture, eating plants or jumping on the dinner table. You may feel like this is an impossible task at first, because cats seem to have a mind of their own. Don't let this fool you. Cats are really highly trainable. They can be trained just like dogs.

The keys to training your cat are positive reinforcement, repetition, and a gentle yet firm attitude. Use tasty treats as positive reinforcement, to reward good behavior. As much as possible, do not use negative reinforcement. To stop unwanted behavior, use something to divert the cat's attention away from what it was doing. Never yell at or hit your pet. At most, you can use a whistle, rattle, or squirt bottle. The idea is to surprise it enough to stop what it was doing, not to frighten it away. If you scare it, it will just run away and hide, without learning that it should not do what it was doing. Be sensible enough to provide a suitable alternative for your cat's unwanted behavior. For example, if you want it to stop scratching the couch, provide it with a scratching post or kitty condo. I personally use a water bottle when one of my cats is doing something bad, and they learn very quickly to stop doing the unwanted behavior. You can also use a certain tone of voice, which cats will soon learn means they are doing something naughty.

You can buy tasty treats for positive reinforcement at any pet store. Or you can make your own. Examples are tuna bits, diced fresh chicken in small cubes, and chicken- or beef-flavored baby food. When your cat does something favorable, like coming to you when you call its name, reward it with a tasty treat. Do this repeatedly, each time it does the desired action.

Here's a sample training technique you can use to teach your cat to sit. The first step is to get its attention. Do this by holding a tasty treat right in front of your cat, near its nose. When it begins to sniff the food, slowly move the treat upwards in an arc (not straight up) from its nose to above its head. Your cat will follow the arc movement with its eyes, raising its chin up and back as it does so, and at the same time moving its butt down on the floor. At the moment it is in the sitting position, praise your pet and give it the tasty treat. You need to be patient, as its butt may not touch the floor on the first few attempts. Just do it again and again until your pet gets it. But remember to be sensible. When your pet gets tired, give it a rest. Repeat the training session another time. It is, in fact, a good idea to keep each training period short. A few minutes usually suffices. If you make it longer than this, the cat will likely just get bored and ignore you.

A useful device to use in training your cat is a clicker. If you don't have one, just use a pen or anything else that makes a clicking sound. Whenever your cat does the correct behavior, use the clicker at that very instant and then offer your cat a treat. It is imperative that you click just at the instant that your cat does the correct behavior. Otherwise, it won't learn to recognize what it is exactly that it did right and should repeat again. When your cat recognizes the behavior you want, it will happily do it again and again.

It is also a good idea to pick your cat up a lot. This gets them used to humans and allows them to be much more friendly over time. In the beginning they may struggle a bit, so giving them a treat after picking them up is a good idea. I pick my cats up all the time and carry them around, and people are always impressed at how friendly they are. Cats prefer to be picked up so that there head is up and there feet are facing the ground. They feel more in control this way. However, we humans tend to love to cradle cats in our arms like a baby. With repeated efforts, you can do this with little problems, just remember that in stressful situations, it is best to pick a cat up under the belly and hold it so that it feels comfortable, otherwise they may use their super strength to break free of your grasp if anything frightens them.

The no-punishment rule bears repeating here. Never hit, shout at, or scare your cat. This is very stressful for the pet, and stress can lead to problem behaviors and even health issues. Overly stressed cats are more prone to diseases such as inflammation of the bladder (called feline idiopathic cystitis). Some signs of stress to watch out for are compulsive grooming, defecating outside the litter box, and hiding away from people.

Like playtime, training is good for your cat (and yourself). To a cat, training it is a great mental workout, as well as a welcome break from long hours of doing nothing in the case of pet owners who are away from home a lot. Trained cats are happier and healthier, and therefore more easy-going. They are also calmer even when their owners are away.

Chapter 8 – How to Keep Your Cat Healthy

To keep your cat healthy, be sure to take it to the veterinarian for its regular vaccinations and check-ups. If you don't have a vet yet, find an animal shelter or rescue group near you, or ask a friend who also owns a pet. It is imperative that your cat be up-to-date with its vaccinations for its own health and safety, and for your own as well. If your pet is sick, it could be spreading viruses that could infect you and your family members. I got my cats from the local animal shelter and I get their vaccinations done there as well for about half the cost of a regular veterinarian.

Many pet owners choose to spay or neuter their cats. This is another health measure that you should discuss with your vet. Another matter you can discuss is pet nutrition. Ask your vet his recommendations on which food items and brands (and in what amounts) are best for your pet's size, age and current health status.

Grooming and cleanliness are also crucial in keeping your cat healthy. While you need to brush your cats fur regularly, you don't need to give it baths as often. Cats clean themselves on their own. But do check for fleas, lumps, and injuries on your cat's skin every now and then, and bring it to the vet as soon as you see something out of the ordinary. If you do need to bathe your cat, ask a family member or friend to assist you. Cats don't like water in general, and they could resist attempts to bathe them. Use cat soap or cat shampoo (not your own), and water that's luke warm. It's also a good idea to put a towel at the bottom of the bathtub for them to grip while bathing. If you can, prior to the bath, put a drop of mineral oil in each of your cat's eyes to prevent soap irritation. Finish bathing it as soon as possible to minimize stress.

The most common cat diseases are diabetes, obesity, kidney disease, cystitis (bladder inflammation), feline asthma, and dental problems. Notice that many of these are directly related to a cat's diet, hence it really is important that the cat is fed properly with nutritious food, rather than just carbohydrate-heavy food.
Diabetic cats may need to be given insulin. This disease poses great difficulties for both the cat and its owner, so ensure that it is prevented as much as possible. Feeding your cat right means, among other things, not over feeding it or giving it a healthier brand of dry cat food. A cat that is obese is prone to diabetes, so try to keep your cat within an ideal weight range. Also, while strictly feeding your cat wet cat food is something they may love, over time this type of diet can lead to serious tooth decay problems which may lead to the vet having to pull out some of their teeth. It is recommended that the majority of a cat's diet be from dry cat food if possible.

Worms are also a common health problem for cats. The symptoms associated with worms are frequent loose stools, a bloated belly, and a malnourished look even with regular, proper diet. Bring your cat to the vet immediately when you see these signs.

Keep a first-aid kit for your cat in case it hurts itself in some accident. A basic kit consists of the following:

- gauze squares
- elastic bandage
- adhesive tape
- eyedroppers
- scissors
- clippers
- tweezers
- penlight flashlight
- gloves (for examining the cat)
- rectal thermometer
- povidone-iodine
- rubbing alcohol (70% isopropyl)
- hydrogen peroxide (3%)
- antiobiotic ointment (examples are neomycin and bacitracin)

You can treat simple wounds and injuries yourself, but bring the cat afterwards to the vet just to be sure. For example, to treat a wound, examine the area for foreign objects that may be imbedded in the wound (such as glass splinters), and remove these with tweezers. Flush the wound with water. Do not apply antiseptics because this will cause the cat pain and it will resist further handling. Then cover the wound with clean gauze. Bring the cat to the vet immediately.

One of a cats and their owners biggest problems is fleas. For some reason fleas love cats, and they can multiply very quickly if swift action is not taken. If you wait too long before trying to fix the problem fleas can spread throughout your whole house. There is nothing worse than when fleas get into your carpet and start chewing up your ankles, or even worse, getting into bed with you. A flea collar is always a good idea, however, these can easily be inadequate. The best flea medicine I have found is by frontline. You put the liquid flea medicine on the back of a cat's neck once a month. I have started doing this at the beginning of spring whether I notice any fleas or not. It is much easier to play it safe, than to go through the nightmare of trying to eliminate fleas once they have spread all throughout your home. I will continue to give them flea medicine once a month until winter has arrived. It is always better to be safe than sorry. You can also try flea powders and flea baths, but I have found these to be much less effective in treating flea problems.

Conclusion

I hope this book was able to help you to learn the basics of cat care, kitten care, play time, nutrition, and training for your cat(s).

The next step is to get a cat or kitten (if you haven't got one yet), and enjoy your time with this wonderfully purr-fect pet. Just follow the steps and strategies discussed in this book and you'll be sure to have a healthy, happy pet to keep you company for many years to come.

Finally, if you discovered at least one thing that has helped you or that you think would be beneficial to someone else, be sure to take a few seconds to easily post a quick positive review. As an author, your positive feedback is desperately needed. Your highly valuable five star reviews are like a river of golden joy flowing through a sunny forest of mighty trees and beautiful flowers! *To do your good deed in making the world a better place by helping others with your valuable insight, just leave a nice review.*

My Other Books and Audio Books
www.AcesEbooks.com

Health Books

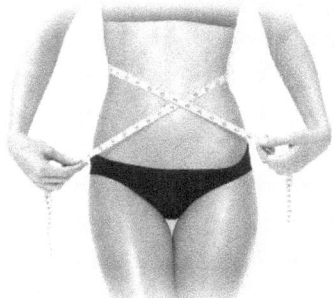

Peak Performance Books

Be sure to check out my audio books as well!

 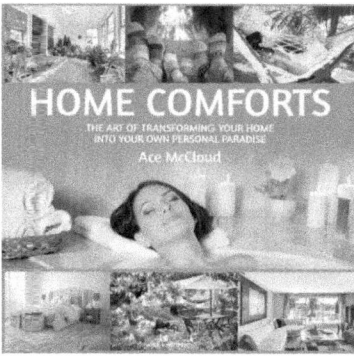 

Check out my website at: **www.AcesEbooks.com** for a complete list of all of my books and high quality audio books. I enjoy bringing you the best knowledge in the world and wish you the best in using this information to make your journey through life better and more enjoyable! **Best of luck to you!**

www.ingramcontent.com/pod-product-compliance
Lightning Source LLC
Chambersburg PA
CBHW051429070526
44584CB00023B/3650